Keep More of Your Money:

Proven Strategies to Minimize Your Taxes

Summary

Are you tired of paying too much in taxes and feeling like you have no control over your finances? Do you want to keep more of your hard-earned money and achieve your financial goals faster? Look no further than our comprehensive guide to minimizing your taxes!

Our book, "**Keep More of Your Money: Proven Strategies to Minimize Your Taxes**," is packed with proven strategies and expert insights to help you reduce your tax burden and keep more of your money. From understanding the tax system to taking advantage of deductions and credits, timing your income and expenses, and hiring a tax professional, we cover all the essential aspects of tax planning.

But we don't stop there. We also explore ethical and legal considerations, helping you approach tax planning with honesty, fairness, and social responsibility. With our guide, you can minimize your taxes while maintaining your integrity and reputation.

With practical tips and step-by-step guidance, you'll be empowered to take control of your finances and achieve your financial goals.

Whether you're a business owner, entrepreneur, or individual looking to minimize your taxes, our guide is the ultimate resource for success. Don't let taxes hold you back - start keeping more of your money today with "**Keep More of Your Money: Proven Strategies to Minimize Your Taxes**."

Introduction
- Importance of minimizing taxes
- Brief overview of tax laws and regulations
- Goals of the book

Chapter 1: Understanding the Tax System
- Overview of how taxes work
- Types of taxes (income, property, sales, etc.)
- Tax brackets and marginal tax rates

Chapter 2: Tax Deductions and Credits
- Overview of tax deductions and credits
- Common deductions and credits
- Strategies for maximizing deductions and credits

Chapter 3: Retirement Accounts and Investments
- Overview of tax-advantaged retirement accounts
- Benefits of contributing to retirement accounts
- Strategies for investing to minimize taxes

Chapter 4: Timing Your Income and Expenses
- Overview of how timing can affect taxes
- Strategies for deferring or accelerating income and expenses
- Rules and regulations

Chapter 5: Charitable Giving
- How charitable donations can reduce taxes
- Types of donations that are tax-deductible
- Strategies for maximizing charitable donations

Introduction

Welcome to the world of taxes, where understanding the tax system is critical to your financial success. Taxes are a necessary part of life, and they fund important programs and services that benefit society. However, it is also essential to minimize taxes to keep more of your hard-earned money.

Paying taxes is an inevitable part of life. While we all understand the importance of contributing to our society's infrastructure and services, it's also essential to ensure that we're not paying more than our fair share. By keeping more of our hard-earned money, we can save for the future, invest in our businesses, and support our families.

The purpose of this book is to provide you with practical strategies for minimizing taxes. Whether you are an individual, a small business owner, or an investor, this book will help you navigate the complex tax system and identify opportunities to reduce your tax burden.

In this book, we will explore different strategies for minimizing taxes, including tax deductions and credits, retirement accounts and investments, business tax strategies, timing your income and expenses, and working with a tax professional. We will also discuss ethical and legal considerations when minimizing taxes.

So, whether you're looking to save on taxes for the first time or want to take your tax planning to the next level, this book is for you. By following the strategies outlined in the following chapters, you'll be on your way to keeping more of your hard-earned money in your pocket.

By the end of this book, you will have a better understanding of the tax system and be equipped with practical strategies for reducing your tax bill. Let's get started!

Chapter 1:

Understanding the Tax System

Taxes are a fundamental part of modern society, and understanding how they work is essential if you want to minimize your tax bill. In this chapter, we'll explore the basics of taxation, including how taxes are calculated, the different types of taxes, and the concept of tax brackets and marginal tax rates.

Overview of how taxes work

At its simplest, a tax is a financial obligation imposed by the government on its citizens or businesses to fund public services and infrastructure. Taxes are typically calculated as a percentage of income, property value, or the price of goods and services, and are paid to the government either directly or through an intermediary like an employer or a bank.

The amount of tax you owe depends on several factors, including your income, your deductions and credits, and the type of tax you're paying. Some taxes are progressive, meaning that the more you earn, the higher the percentage of tax you pay, while others are regressive, meaning that everyone pays the same percentage of tax regardless of income.

Different Types of Taxes

There are many different types of taxes, each with its own set of rules and regulations. The most common types of taxes include:

- **Income Tax**

This is a tax on the money you earn from working or investments. Income tax rates are usually progressive, meaning that the more you earn, the higher the percentage of tax you pay.

- **Property Tax**

This is a tax on the value of real estate or personal property that you own. Property tax rates vary by state and locality.

- **Sales Tax**

This is a tax on the price of goods and services that you purchase. Sales tax rates also vary by state and locality.

- **Payroll Tax**

This is a tax on the wages and salaries paid by employers to their employees. Payroll taxes fund Social Security and Medicare.

- **Estate Tax**

This is a tax on the value of an individual's assets at the time of their death. Estate tax only applies to estates above a certain value.

Tax Brackets and Marginal Tax Rates

One of the most important concepts to understand when it comes to taxes is tax brackets and marginal tax rates. Tax brackets are ranges of income to which a specific tax rate applies. The more you earn, the higher your tax rate will be. Marginal tax rates refer to the tax rate you pay on each additional dollar of income you earn.

For example, let's say you're a single taxpayer with an income of $50,000. In 2023, the IRS tax brackets for single taxpayers are as follows:

- ★ 10% on income up to $10,275
- ★ 12% on income between $10,276 and $41,775
- ★ 22% on income between $41,776 and $91,525
- ★ 24% on income between $91,526 and $191,500
- ★ 32% on income between $191,501 and $416,700
- ★ 35% on income between $416,701 and $418,400
- ★ 37% on income over $418,400

Based on these tax brackets, your marginal tax rate would be 22%, which means that any additional income you earn above $50,000 would be taxed at a rate of 22%.

Understanding tax brackets and marginal tax rates is important because it can help you make informed decisions about how to manage your income and taxes. For example, you may want to consider contributing to a tax-deferred retirement account to reduce your taxable income and lower your tax bracket.

In conclusion, understanding the basics of taxation is essential if you want to minimize your tax bill. By having a clear understanding of how taxes work and the different types of taxes, you can make informed decisions about your finances and take advantage of the various tax-saving strategies available to you. In the following chapters, we'll explore some of the most effective ways to minimize your taxes, from deductions and credits to retirement accounts and business tax strategies.

Chapter 2:

Tax Deductions and Credits

When it comes to minimizing your taxes, deductions and credits can be your best friend. Deductions reduce your taxable income, while credits directly reduce the amount of tax you owe. In this chapter, we'll explore some of the most common deductions and credits available to taxpayers, including those related to healthcare, education, and charitable giving.

Standard Deduction vs. Itemized Deduction

Before we dive into specific deductions, it's important to understand the difference between the standard deduction and itemized deduction. The standard deduction is a set amount that you can deduct from your taxable income without having to provide specific documentation. For 2023, the standard deduction for a single taxpayer is $12,850, while for married couples filing jointly, it's $25,700.

On the other hand, itemized deductions require you to provide specific documentation of expenses related to things like healthcare, charitable giving, and state and local taxes. You'll only want to itemize your deductions if they add up to more than the standard deduction.

Healthcare Deductions and Credits

Healthcare expenses can be a significant burden, but the IRS offers several deductions and credits to help alleviate the financial strain. Here are some of the most common healthcare-related tax breaks:

- **Medical Expenses Deduction**

You can deduct the cost of medical expenses that exceed 7.5% of your adjusted gross income (AGI). This can include things like doctor visits, prescription medication, and medical equipment.

- **Health Savings Account (HSA) Deduction**

If you have a high-deductible health plan (HDHP), you can contribute to an HSA and deduct those contributions from your taxable income. HSA funds can be used to pay for qualified medical expenses tax-free.

- **Premium Tax Credit**

If you purchase health insurance through the marketplace, you may be eligible for a premium tax credit that reduces the cost of your monthly premiums.

Education Deductions and Credits

Education can be a significant expense, but the IRS offers several deductions and credits to help offset the cost. Here are some of the most common education-related tax breaks:

- **Student Loan Interest Deduction**

You can deduct up to $2,500 in student loan interest paid during the year.

- **American Opportunity Tax Credit (AOTC)**

The AOTC provides a tax credit of up to $2,500 per eligible student for qualified education expenses, including tuition, fees, and course materials.

- **Lifetime Learning Credit**

The Lifetime Learning Credit provides a tax credit of up to $2,000 per tax return for qualified education expenses.

Charitable Deductions and Credits

Giving to charity not only helps others, but it can also provide a tax break. Here are some of the most common charitable deductions and credits:

- **Charitable Contributions Deduction**
You can deduct cash and non-cash donations to qualified charitable organizations, up to 60% of your AGI.

- **Charitable Mileage Deduction**
If you volunteer for a charitable organization and use your car for transportation, you can deduct the mileage at a rate of 14 cents per mile.

- **Charitable Giving Tax Credit**
Some states offer tax credits for charitable giving. Check with your state to see if you're eligible.

In conclusion, deductions and credits can be powerful tools in minimizing your tax bill. By taking advantage of the deductions and credits available to you, you can significantly reduce the amount of tax you owe and keep more of your hard-earned money in your pocket.

Chapter 3:

Retirement Accounts and Investments

Retirement accounts offer an excellent way to save for retirement while minimizing your taxes. Not only do these accounts offer tax-deferred growth, but they also offer several tax benefits that can significantly reduce your tax bill. In this chapter, we'll explore some of the most common retirement accounts available to taxpayers, including 401(k)s, IRAs, and SEP-IRAs.

401(k)s

A 401(k) is a retirement account offered by many employers. Contributions to a 401(k) are made with pre-tax dollars, which means that you don't have to pay taxes on the money until you withdraw it in retirement. Additionally, many employers offer matching contributions, which can significantly increase the amount of money you save.

For 2023, the maximum contribution limit for a 401(k) is $20,500 for those under 50 years old, and $27,000 for those 50 years or older.

IRAs

Individual Retirement Accounts (IRAs) are retirement accounts that individuals can open on their own. There are two types of IRAs: traditional IRAs and Roth IRAs.

- **Traditional IRA**

Contributions to a traditional IRA are made with pre-tax dollars, just like a 401(k). This means that you don't have to pay taxes on the money until you withdraw it in retirement. For 2023, the maximum contribution limit for a traditional IRA is $6,000 for those under 50 years old, and $7,000 for those 50 years or older.

- **Roth IRA**

Contributions to a Roth IRA are made with after-tax dollars. This means that you don't get a tax break when you contribute, but your withdrawals in retirement are tax-free. For 2023, the maximum contribution limit for a Roth IRA is $6,000 for those under 50 years old, and $7,000 for those 50 years or older.

SEP-IRAs

A Simplified Employee Pension (SEP) IRA is a retirement account that is designed for self-employed individuals and small business owners. SEP-IRAs offer tax-deferred growth, and contributions are made with pre-tax dollars.

For 2023, the maximum contribution limit for a SEP-IRA is 25% of compensation or $61,000, whichever is less.

Other Retirement Accounts

In addition to the retirement accounts mentioned above, there are several other retirement accounts available to taxpayers, including:

- Solo 401(k): A retirement account designed for self-employed individuals.

- Simple IRA: A retirement account designed for small businesses.

- 403(b): A retirement account offered by non-profit organizations.

Benefits of Retirement Accounts

Retirement accounts offer several benefits, including:

- **Tax-deferred growth**
Your investments grow tax-free until you withdraw the money in retirement.

- **Tax deductions**

Contributions to traditional IRAs, 401(k)s, and other retirement accounts are tax-deductible, reducing your taxable income.

- **Employer contributions**

Many employers offer matching contributions to 401(k) accounts, which can significantly increase your savings.

In conclusion, retirement accounts offer an excellent way to save for retirement while minimizing your taxes. By taking advantage of the various retirement accounts available to you, you can significantly reduce your tax bill and secure a comfortable retirement.

Investment Strategies

Investment strategies can also provide tax benefits. One strategy is to invest in tax-free municipal bonds, which provide tax-free income. Another strategy is to invest in tax-deferred annuities, which allow your investment to grow tax-free until you start taking withdrawals.

Timing of Withdrawals

When it comes to retirement accounts, timing is key. It's important to understand the rules for withdrawing funds from your retirement accounts to avoid penalties and taxes. Generally, withdrawals from retirement accounts before age 59 1/2 are subject to a 10% penalty, in addition to income tax. However, there are exceptions, such as for certain medical expenses or first-time homebuyers.

Understanding retirement accounts and investment strategies can help you maximize tax benefits and minimize taxes. In the next section, we will explore business tax strategies, which can provide additional opportunities for reducing your tax bill.

"In this world, nothing can be said to be certain, except death and taxes."

~ Benjamin Franklin

Chapter 4:

Timing Your Income and Expenses

Timing your income and expenses is another effective way to minimize taxes. In this section, we will explore some general tips for timing your income and expenses to reduce your tax liability.

- **Accelerating Deductions**

Accelerating deductions means taking deductions in the current year rather than waiting until the following year. This strategy can be effective if you expect your tax rate to be higher in the current year. For example, you can prepay some of your business expenses, such as rent or utilities, in the current year to take advantage of the deduction.

- **Deferring Income**

Deferring income means delaying receipt of income until the following year. This strategy can be effective if you expect your tax rate to be lower in the following year. For example, you can delay invoicing clients until the following year to reduce your taxable income for the current year.

- **Timing Capital Gains and Losses**

Capital gains and losses are taxed differently than ordinary income. Long-term capital gains are taxed at a lower rate than short-term capital gains, and capital losses can be used to offset capital gains. Timing the sale of capital assets can help you maximize your tax benefits.

- **Charitable Contributions**

Charitable contributions can provide tax benefits, but the timing of the contribution can affect the size of the deduction. By timing your contributions, you can maximize your tax benefits. For example, you can make a contribution at the end of the year to take advantage of the deduction for the current year.

- **Filing Status**

Finally, your filing status can also affect your tax liability. Married couples who file jointly may pay less in taxes than those who file separately. In addition, if you are eligible for head of household status, you may be able to take advantage of a lower tax rate.

Timing your income and expenses can be an effective way to minimize taxes. By understanding the rules and regulations, you can make informed decisions that will reduce your tax liability. In the next section, we will summarize the key points and provide some additional resources for minimizing taxes.

Chapter 5:

Charitable Giving

Charitable giving is not only a great way to give back to the community, but it can also provide several tax benefits. In this chapter, we'll explore some of the ways that charitable giving can help you minimize your taxes.

Tax Deductions for Charitable Contributions

When you make a charitable contribution, you may be eligible for a tax deduction. The amount of the deduction depends on the type of donation you make and your income level.

- **Cash Donations**

If you make a cash donation to a qualified charitable organization, you may be able to deduct the full amount of the donation on your taxes, up to 60% of your adjusted gross income (AGI).

- **Non-Cash Donations**

If you make a non-cash donation, such as donating clothes or household items to a charitable organization, you can deduct the fair market value of the items on your taxes.

- **Donating Appreciated Assets**

If you donate appreciated assets, such as stocks or real estate, you can deduct the fair market value of the assets on your taxes and avoid paying capital gains taxes on the appreciation.

Donor-Advised Funds

A donor-advised fund is a charitable giving vehicle that allows you to make a charitable contribution and receive an immediate tax deduction, while also retaining the ability to recommend where the funds are distributed over time. This can be a great way to maximize your tax deduction while also having control over how your donation is used.

Charitable Trusts

Charitable trusts are another way to make charitable contributions while minimizing your taxes. There are two types of charitable trusts: charitable remainder trusts and charitable lead trusts.

- **Charitable Remainder Trusts**

A charitable remainder trust allows you to donate assets to a charitable organization while retaining an income stream from those assets. You receive an immediate tax deduction for the charitable contribution, and you can receive income from the assets for a specified period of time.

- **Charitable Lead Trusts**

A charitable lead trust is the opposite of a charitable remainder trust. With a charitable lead trust, the charitable organization receives income from the assets for a specified period of time, and then the assets are transferred to the beneficiary.

Volunteer Work

In addition to making monetary donations, volunteer work can also provide tax benefits. While you cannot deduct the value of your time, you can deduct certain expenses associated with volunteering, such as transportation costs and supplies.

Corporate Charitable Giving

If you own a business, charitable giving can also provide tax benefits. Corporations can deduct up to 10% of their taxable income for charitable contributions, and excess contributions can be carried forward for up to five years.

In conclusion, charitable giving can be an effective way to minimize your taxes while also making a positive impact in your community. By taking advantage of the various charitable giving strategies available to you, you can make the most of your donations and reduce your tax bill.

Chapter 6:

Business Tax Strategies

If you own a business, you have many opportunities to minimize your taxes by taking advantage of various tax deductions and credits. In this chapter, we'll explore some of the most effective business tax strategies.

Deductible Business Expenses

One of the most effective ways to minimize your business taxes is to take advantage of deductible business expenses. Deductible expenses include any expenses that are ordinary and necessary for your business, such as office supplies, travel expenses, and employee salaries.

- **Home Office Deduction**

If you work from home, you may be eligible for a home office deduction. This deduction allows you to deduct a portion of your home expenses, such as mortgage interest, property taxes, and utilities, as a business expense.

- **Retirement Plan Contributions**

Contributing to a retirement plan, such as a 401(k) or a SEP IRA, can also help minimize your taxes. These contributions are tax-deductible and can help reduce your taxable income.

Business Tax Credits

In addition to deductions, there are also various tax credits available to businesses. Tax credits provide a dollar-for-dollar reduction in your tax bill and can be extremely valuable.

- **Research and Development Tax Credit**

The research and development tax credit is designed to encourage businesses to invest in research and development activities. This credit can be claimed for expenses related to developing new products, improving existing products, and developing new manufacturing processes.

- **Work Opportunity Tax Credit**

The work opportunity tax credit provides a tax credit for businesses that hire individuals from certain targeted groups, such as veterans and ex-felons.

Entity Selection

The type of entity you choose for your business can also have a significant impact on your taxes. There are several types of entities to choose from, including sole proprietorships, partnerships, S corporations, and C corporations.

- **Pass-Through Entities**

Pass-through entities, such as sole proprietorships, partnerships, and S corporations, do not pay income taxes at the business level. Instead, the income is passed through to the owners and taxed at their individual tax rates.

- **C Corporations**

C corporations, on the other hand, pay income taxes at the business level and may be subject to double taxation. However, C corporations may be able to take advantage of certain deductions and credits that are not available to pass-through entities.

Tax Planning

Effective tax planning can also help minimize your business taxes. Tax planning involves analyzing your business's finances and identifying opportunities to reduce your tax bill.

- **Timing of Income and Expenses**

One effective tax planning strategy is to time your income and expenses to minimize your tax liability. For example, you may want to defer income until the following year or accelerate expenses to the current year.

- **Depreciation**

Depreciation is the process of deducting the cost of business assets over time. By taking advantage of depreciation, you can reduce your taxable income and minimize your taxes.

In conclusion, there are many effective business tax strategies available to business owners. By taking advantage of deductible expenses, tax credits, entity selection, and tax planning strategies, you can minimize your taxes and keep more of your hard-earned money.

Chapter 7:

Real Estate Strategies

Real estate is a popular investment for many people, and it can also provide valuable tax benefits. In this chapter, we'll explore some of the most effective real estate tax strategies.

Depreciation

One of the most significant tax benefits of owning real estate is depreciation. Depreciation is the process of deducting the cost of the property over time. This deduction can be taken even if the property is appreciating in value, making it a valuable tax benefit for real estate investors.

1031 Exchange

A 1031 exchange is a tax-deferred exchange that allows real estate investors to sell a property and reinvest the proceeds in a new property without paying capital gains taxes. To qualify for a 1031 exchange, the properties must be used for business or investment purposes.

Rental Property Tax Deductions

If you own rental property, you may be eligible for various tax deductions. These deductions can include expenses such as mortgage interest, property taxes, repairs, and maintenance. You may also be able to deduct depreciation and the cost of travel expenses related to managing your rental property.

Real Estate Professional Status

If you are a real estate professional, you may be able to deduct all of your real estate losses against your other income, including wages and salaries. To qualify as a real estate professional, you must spend at least 750 hours per year on real estate activities and more than half of your working time on real estate activities.

Vacation Home Rental

If you own a vacation home, you may be able to rent it out and take advantage of valuable tax benefits. Rental income can be offset by deductions such as mortgage interest, property taxes, and depreciation. However, it's essential to understand the rules around vacation home rental to ensure that you meet the requirements for tax deductions.

Real Estate Investment Trusts (REITs)

Real Estate Investment Trusts (REITs) are companies that own or finance income-producing real estate. By investing in a REIT, you can take advantage of the tax benefits of owning real estate without the hassles of property management.

In conclusion, real estate can provide valuable tax benefits for investors. By taking advantage of depreciation, 1031 exchanges, rental property tax deductions, real estate professional status, vacation home rental, and REITs, you can minimize your taxes and keep more of your hard-earned money. However, it's essential to understand the rules and requirements for each of these strategies to ensure that you are taking advantage of all available tax benefits.

"A penny saved is a penny earned."

~ Benjamin Franklin

Chapter 8:

Tax Planning and Preparation

Proper tax planning and preparation are essential to minimize your taxes and ensure that you comply with all tax laws and regulations. In this chapter, we'll explore some tips for effective tax planning and preparation.

Start Early

The earlier you start your tax planning and preparation, the better. By starting early, you'll have more time to gather all the necessary documents and information, identify potential deductions and credits, and plan your tax strategy effectively.

Keep Accurate Records

Keeping accurate records is crucial for effective tax planning and preparation. You should keep records of all income, expenses, and deductions throughout the year. By keeping accurate records, you'll have all the information you need to file your taxes correctly and take advantage of all available deductions and credits.

Hire a Professional

If your taxes are complicated, or you're unsure about how to prepare your taxes, consider hiring a professional tax preparer. A tax professional can help you identify potential deductions and credits, ensure that you comply with all tax laws and regulations, and help you minimize your taxes.

Use Tax Software

If you prefer to prepare your taxes yourself, consider using tax software. Tax software can help you identify potential deductions and credits, guide you through the tax preparation process, and help you file your taxes electronically.

Plan for Next Year

Effective tax planning doesn't just happen during tax season. You should also plan for the upcoming tax year throughout the year. By planning ahead, you can take advantage of available tax benefits, maximize your deductions and credits, and minimize your taxes.

Stay Informed

Tax laws and regulations change frequently, so it's essential to stay informed about any changes that may affect your taxes. You can stay informed by reading tax publications, attending tax seminars, and consulting with a tax professional.

In conclusion, effective tax planning and preparation are essential to minimize your taxes and ensure that you comply with all tax laws and regulations. By starting early, keeping accurate records, hiring a professional, using tax software, planning for next year, and staying informed, you can minimize your taxes and keep more of your hard-earned money.

"Do not save what is left after spending;
instead, spend what is left after saving."

~ Warren Buffett

Chapter 9:

Hiring a Tax Professional

Minimizing taxes can be a complex and time-consuming process. Hiring a tax professional can help ensure that you are taking advantage of all available tax strategies and avoiding costly mistakes. In this section, we will explore the benefits of hiring a tax professional and provide some tips for finding the right one.

Benefits of Hiring a Tax Professional

- **Expertise**

Tax professionals have the knowledge and experience to navigate complex tax laws and regulations.

- **Time Savings**

Hiring a tax professional can free up your time to focus on other areas of your business.

- **Minimize Errors**

Tax professionals can help you avoid mistakes that could result in penalties or additional taxes.

- **Maximizing Deductions**

A tax professional can help you identify all available deductions and credits to minimize your tax liability.

Tips for Finding the Right Tax Professional

- **Credentials**

Look for a tax professional with relevant credentials, such as a Certified Public Accountant (CPA) or Enrolled Agent (EA).

- **Experience**

Find a tax professional with experience working with clients in your industry or with similar tax situations.

- **Communication**

Choose a tax professional who communicates clearly and promptly.

- **Fees**

Consider the fees charged by the tax professional and make sure they are reasonable for the services provided.

In conclusion, hiring a tax professional can be a valuable investment in minimizing your taxes. By leveraging their expertise and experience, you can take advantage of all available tax strategies and avoid costly mistakes. In the final section, we will provide some additional resources for minimizing taxes.

Chapter 10:

Ethical and Legal Considerations

When it comes to minimizing taxes, it is important to consider both ethical and legal considerations. In this section, we will explore some key considerations to keep in mind.

Ethical Considerations

- **Honesty**

It is important to be honest in your tax reporting and not engage in any fraudulent or deceptive practices.

- **Fairness**

While it is legal to minimize your taxes, it is important to do so in a fair and equitable manner.

- **Social Responsibility**

Consider the impact of your tax strategies on society and the broader community.

Legal Considerations

- **Compliance**

Ensure that your tax strategies are in compliance with all applicable laws and regulations.

- **Documentation**

Keep accurate and complete records to support your tax deductions and credits.

- **Disclosure**

Disclose all relevant information to the IRS and other tax authorities.

It is important to work with a tax professional who adheres to ethical and legal standards. Avoid engaging in any questionable tax strategies that may be viewed as abusive or fraudulent by the IRS.

By keeping these considerations in mind, you can minimize your taxes while maintaining your integrity and reputation.

In conclusion, minimizing taxes requires careful planning and consideration of various strategies and factors. By understanding the tax system, taking advantage of deductions and credits, timing your income and expenses, hiring a tax professional, and adhering to ethical and legal standards, you can minimize your tax liability and keep more of your hard-earned money.

Conclusion

Taxes are an unavoidable part of life, but they don't have to be a burden. By implementing effective tax strategies and planning, you can minimize your taxes and keep more of your hard-earned money. In this ebook, we've explored some proven strategies for minimizing your taxes, including:

- Understanding taxes and how they work
- Taking advantage of deductions and credits
- Utilizing retirement accounts
- Making charitable contributions
- Implementing business tax strategies
- Leveraging real estate tax benefits
- Effective tax planning and preparation

By implementing these strategies, you can minimize your taxes and keep more of your money in your pocket. However, it's essential to remember that tax laws and regulations are constantly changing, so it's essential to stay informed and consult with a tax professional.

With the right approach and guidance, you can minimize your taxes while maintaining your integrity and reputation. Remember, every dollar saved in taxes is a dollar that can be reinvested in your business or used to achieve your financial goals.

In conclusion, minimizing your taxes requires effort and planning, but it can be done. By taking advantage of available tax benefits and implementing effective tax strategies, you can reduce your tax liability and keep more of your hard-earned money. Remember to stay informed, plan ahead, and consult with a tax professional to ensure that you're taking advantage of all available tax benefits.

<u>With the right approach, you can keep more of your money and achieve your financial goals!</u>

FAQ

What is tax minimization, and why is it important?
Tax minimization is the process of legally reducing your tax liability to keep more of your money. It's essential because taxes can be a significant financial burden, and minimizing them can help you achieve your financial goals faster.

Are tax minimization strategies legal?
Yes, tax minimization strategies are legal. They involve taking advantage of available tax benefits and incentives to reduce your tax liability.

How can I reduce my tax liability?
You can reduce your tax liability by utilizing deductions and credits, contributing to retirement accounts, making charitable contributions, implementing business tax strategies, and taking advantage of real estate tax benefits, among other strategies.

Do I need a professional to help me with tax minimization?
While you can implement tax minimization strategies on your own, it's often helpful to work with a tax professional. A professional can provide guidance on the most effective strategies for your situation and ensure that you're taking advantage of all available tax benefits.

How far in advance should I start tax planning?

It's best to start tax planning as early as possible, ideally at the beginning of the tax year. This will give you plenty of time to implement effective strategies and ensure that you're prepared for tax season.

What is a tax deduction, and how does it work?

A tax deduction is an expense that can be subtracted from your taxable income, reducing your tax liability. For example, if you make a charitable contribution of $1,000 and your tax rate is 25%, you could receive a $250 tax deduction.

What is a tax credit, and how does it work?

A tax credit is a dollar-for-dollar reduction of your tax liability. For example, if you have a tax liability of $1,000 and you're eligible for a $500 tax credit, your tax liability would be reduced to $500.

Can I deduct business expenses on my personal tax return?

Yes, if you're a sole proprietor or a freelancer, you can deduct business expenses on your personal tax return using Schedule C.

How can real estate be used as a tax minimization strategy?

Real estate can be used as a tax minimization strategy by taking advantage of tax benefits such as the mortgage interest deduction and the property tax deduction. Additionally, real estate investors can use strategies such as 1031 exchanges to defer taxes on capital gains.

What are some common mistakes to avoid when implementing tax minimization strategies?

Common mistakes to avoid when implementing tax minimization strategies include failing to keep accurate records, missing tax deadlines, and failing to consult with a tax professional. It's important to stay informed and ensure that you're implementing strategies correctly to avoid potential penalties and fines.